TO RELATE after TRAUMA

Developing and Using Survival Tools to Live on 'Life's Terms'

G U I D E B O O K
REVISED EDITION

A TONIER CAIN INTERNATIONAL PUBLICATION

TCI PUBLISHING HOUSE

Copyright © 2019 by Tonier Cain International
Revised May 2022

All rights reserved. Printed in the United States of America. No part of this booklet may be reproduced, scanned or distributed in any printed or electronic form without permission. Please do not participate in or encourage piracy of copyrighted materials in violation of the author's rights. Purchase only authorized editions.

Healing Neen, Tonier Cain International and its logos are trademarks of Tonier Cain International, Inc.

A Tonier Cain International Publication
P.O. Box 175 • Arnold, MD 21012

Author: Tonier Cain
Editor: Desiráe G. Wright
Cover Design, Interior Layout: Christopher K. Wright

*Father in Heaven,
I thank you for your healing and your
deliverance. I ask, Father, that you
guide our steps, our hearts, and our
spirits as we learn to live on life's terms.*

*Father, I ask that you bless
every one that reads this book
seeking inspiration and hope.*

*Let it be as such. May you be glorified,
as you so deserve.*

*I ask this in our precious Lord
and Savior, Jesus Christ.*

Amen.

ACKNOWLEDGEMENTS

First and always, I want to give thanks to God for the wisdom he has given to me and those that contributed to this guide, inspired by the spirit of God, I am confident this guide will help many survivors and bring much glory to God, our Father in Heaven.

A very special thank you to those that contributed:

Dr. Neil Boris, Circle of Security International
Orlandra Foote
Natasha Wills
Adrian Muldrow
LaTonya Edwards
Your expertise and stories brought even more light to this book.

Desirae Wright, who turned our stories into a life-changing guidebook.

Jamellah Sweeting and Donna Sweeting, for your editing input.

Lisa Tabler for gathering inspirational scriptures.

Christopher Wright, for his amazing layout and graphic design work.

And finally, to those that will use this guide, I thank you for allowing us to use our stories to inspire you to find, develop and maintain healthy relationships.

CONTENTS

INTRODUCTION			i
CHAPTER	1	**IDENTIFYING A TRAUMATIC PAST**	1
CHAPTER	2	**MOTHERHOOD**	7
CHAPTER	3	**EMPLOYEE**	29
CHAPTER	4	**DATING**	35
CHAPTER	5	**MARRIAGE**	51
CHAPTER	6	**FRIENDSHIP**	65
CHAPTER	7	**BUSINESS OWNER**	73
CHAPTER	8	**CHILD OF GOD**	81
APPENDIX			99
PREVALENCE OF TRAUMA			101
SIGNS OF TRAUMA			103
GLOSSARY OF TRAUMA-INFORMED TERMS			105
RESOURCES AND REFERENCES			109
ABOUT THE AUTHOR			115

INTRODUCTION

In 2014, I released my autobiography titled *Healing Neen,* a brutally honest account of endless abuse, neglect, and pain. As a child I suffered at the hands of adults tasked with the responsibility of caring for me. I was abused by my ex-husband, correctional officers, police, drug dealers, counselors, judges and men I met while prostituting to feed my drug habit. I bore four children during this dark time, losing them all in various ways. I lied, cheated, and stole to get by. I spent 19 years on the mean streets of Annapolis, Md., with no place to call home. Part of the time, I lived under a bridge. I was arrested 83 times, convicted 66 times.

Miraculously, I eventually healed, thanks to people that showed me kindness and believed in me when I didn't believe in myself. Most of all, I turned to a never-failing, always-forgiving and generous God. I thought God would surely have nothing to do with a lost soul like me. I was beyond redemption, or so I thought. Bit by bit positive changes, large and small occurred in my life after I looked to the Lord. The same Lord I rejected over and over again earlier in my life.

By far the biggest and most important change occurred the day I learned about a program to help pregnant women in prison. That was me! I tried to enroll in the trauma therapy program, but I was turned down because I hadn't been in jail long enough to qualify. I wanted to enroll in this program so much, that I asked to have my prison sentence extended! My wish was granted. I got into the program. It was the best thing to happen to me because it looked deep into my tortured past and allowed me to slowly shed the hundreds of shameful episodes I endured. I was taught that all the bad things I kept blaming on myself were really the fault of those who neglected me, abused me, abandoned me, time after time after time. Other programs only dealt with my outward behaviors, instead of the demons I buried deep within me for decades. As I wrote in *Healing Neen,* "Those therapists tried to put good on top of the poop in my life. When you do that, all you have is poop with whipped cream on top."

The therapy-informed program in tandem with the work God was doing within, did so much more for me. It's not an easy program. Some of the pain walled off for years was almost too hard to confront. However, my caring therapists always let me move at my own pace. They never let me forget I was the victim in all this, not an inherently evil person. Over time, I regained my pride, had a fifth child, Orlandra (now a teen) and moved into my own home. I married a man who is extremely supportive and loves me, unlike my manipulative and mean first husband I divorced. Professionally, I started a business to share the wonders of trauma-based therapy with companies and organizations across the globe.

I wrote this guide book to explore how to keep surviving a traumatic background in many settings – as a mother, as an employee, as someone active on the dating scene, as a person undertaking marriage again, as a friend, as a business owner, and – critically – as a child of God. This book also includes the words of others who have gone down the same dark roads I've traveled, telling how they managed to emerge.

I hope their thoughts and mine reach those struggling with a life that seems hopeless, with problems they think too great to conquer, with a darkness so heavy they believe it will never lift. With God at our side and His desire to lift up even the most wretched among us, I am sure it will happen. Get your journal and let's move towards healing, together. Journaling is required to fully benefit from this guide book.

Where there's breath, there's hope!

I will pray for each of you always, and I ask God to give you peace, joy, healing – His healing! – and the strength to forgive yourself and others. So be blessed and encouraged. God is able! I love each and every one of you.

1

IDENTIFYING A TRAUMATIC PAST

—

"Then the peace of God that exceeds all understanding will keep your hearts and minds safe in Christ Jesus."

PHILIPPIANS 4:7

Trauma is all too common these days, or maybe it's just that more people are talking about it. You can't turn on the news, or scroll on Facebook or Twitter, without reading or hearing about someone's trauma. Below are some ways trauma survivors may be affected by the increase of social attention it's getting these days:

- How we view the world around us
- How we parent our children
- How we deal with 'triggers'

THE WORLD AROUND ME

All of my past sexual abuse is now what I see and hear on TV and read on social media. Then there's the #metoo movement that confirms danger is everywhere. Every day trauma survivors wake up to a world that may remind us of what we've endured. We must work, go to school, take care of our families, attend church, and interact with friends. The sentence, "Life goes on as usual." applies to all our lives, but life for those of us who have been abused and traumatized is never 'as usual.'

PARENTING

If I see a news alert about a sexual predator on the loose, the fear for my daughter becomes overwhelming, even though the sexual predator is in California and I'm in Maryland, thousands of miles away. I feel as if it's my next-door neighbor.

I need to do all I can to makes sure my daughter is safe. Something I do is, go into her room, sit on her bed and strike up a conversation. Hoping she doesn't see the fear in my eyes, I hug her and go into my safety talk. She's heard it so many times, but I want to make sure she's aware and equipped. She could probably tell me word-for-word what I am about to say. I try very hard not to cause fear in her, but sometimes it can't be helped.

BEING TRIGGERED

As a trauma survivor, the increased social attention being given to trauma, takes me back to my own traumatic past quite frequently. I begin to get lost in the sea of anguish again. All that I'm reading and hearing every day requires the use of my healthy coping tools daily.

There are other times when my heart seems to stop -- if I hear a voice that sounds like someone who has hurt me. Even the smell of a certain cologne might trigger me. I'm triggered often, when it happens, I go directly into my toolkit to grab a tool to help me self-regulate. Learning how to self-regulate is vital for trauma survivors to enjoy a healthy life. My toolkit is uniquely tailored to fit me and my lifestyle, and yours should be too.

JOURNAL ASSIGNMENT #1

- Divide the page in two.
- On the left side list, your triggers.
- On the right side, list the tools you use to deal with each trigger.

Be honest with yourself. This is an exercise to help, not judge. It's alright if you don't know what triggers you or how to self-regulate. You can start identifying them now.

When you're faced with something that causes you fear, puts your senses on alert or kicks you into fight or flight mode; that's a trigger. Add it to your list.

What you find yourself doing after you've been triggered is how you cope. Add it to your list, then evaluate if your method of coping is healthy.

(See list of internet resources in the back)

We must maneuver our way around and through our triggers. Although we go through a great deal of healing, we never forget. Life after trauma is different. We are always alert, often scared, and always ready to fight. It becomes our 'survival mode.' But if this survival mode is not maintained in a healthy way, it can lead us into very unhealthy relationships.

Let's talk about some of these relationships.

2

MOTHERHOOD

—

"Don't be anxious about anything: Rather, bring up all of your requests to God in prayer and petitions, along with giving thanks."

PHILIPPIANS 4:6

IMPORTANT DEFINITIONS
(DICTIONARY.COM)

- Motherhood: *(noun)* the state of being a mother
- Mother: *(noun)* a female parent
- Parent: *(noun)* father or mother
- Parent: *(verb)* raise, bring up, look after, take care of

As I started to think about what I wanted to write regarding this chapter, I decided to look up the definition of motherhood, which led me to look up mother. No surprises with those definitions. However, the verb form of parent described a nurturing and loving person which was unfamiliar to me. Parenting is something I'm constantly battling to master.

Things that influence our perspectives on parenting:

- How well we were parented
- What a mother or father looks like to us

MY CHILDHOOD RELATIONSHIP WITH MY PARENTS

I was raised in a household where there was very little or no protection, nurturing, or love. I realized early in life that my survival depended on me. I had to look out for myself. I knew someone gave birth to me, but I never experience a mother, in the verb sense. Nobody 'looked after' or 'took care of' me. I was in a really bad situation growing up. Surrounded by abandonment and neglect. Everyone that was supposed to take care of me seemed to hurt or harm me repeatedly, in a variety of ways. From my mother, leaving me alone and hungry in the house, while she ate with neighbors. To my father, who left without explanation when I was very young. I have few memories of him being in my life as a child. As a learning creature, I absorbed what I witnessed in my immediate environment. We all have unique experiences and are affected by the overall atmosphere of our communities.

HOW THAT RELATIONSHIP SHAPED MY PERSPECTIVES

Not receiving true parenting in my life caused me to lack self-esteem and hope. I believed I was nothing, would never amount to anything, and that's just how it was going to be. This negative belief system is what I lived by. I was a child that desperately needed a parent. When I married a much older man, I thought he could be my husband and parent. Does this seem odd or strange to you? Remember, a parent (noun) is simply a father or mother, but to mother or to father (verb) means to actively care for and look after children, to nurture.

That's what I was hoping for in my husband. He was in his mid-twenties, eight years older than me. I was a teenager with very few useful life lessons to bring to a marriage. I looked for my husband to be my protector. He would be the one that looked after me and took care of me, but that didn't happen. Our relationship quickly turned violent and abusive.

I viewed mother and motherhood as merely giving birth, which was effortless for me. I never knew more than that. I never felt more than that. My perspective led me to give birth to 5 kids. Pushing out babies became easy. But the difficulty came with knowing how to love and nurture.

THE BEGINNING OF MY RELATIONSHIP WITH MOTHERHOOD

As I grew older, nothing seemed to change the way I felt about motherhood. Nothing within me seemed to be a nurturing and loving parent. My traumatic childhood impaired my ability to separate my troubled past, from being a true mother. When I gave birth to my first son, I hoped he would fill my emotional void, even though he was just an infant. I thought he would be the one to love me.

It's true that children love unconditionally, but it's not the kind of nuanced and sympathetic love we all learn later and need. No matter how often my mother failed to parent me in a nurturing way, I still loved her. Even when I lived through her steady neglect and abuse, I somehow managed to love her at some level, in some way. Because of this I knew, no matter what happened, my son would love me. I depended on his love for my survival. This is not as it should have been.

I clung to that baby and needed him to love me unconditionally. Up to that point, any love I received had conditions and consequences.

When my son turned 2 years old, my husband decided to remove him from my care. That caused me to seek out ways to cope with the resulting trauma and despair. My son was gone, snatched from me, just like that, no warning. Not only did I have to deal with my traumatic youth, but now a fresh layer of trauma was added – the sudden loss of my first-born son.

> **JOURNAL ASSIGNMENT #2**
>
> We are not responsible for the voids caused in our lives; however we have the power to fill them in healthy ways. Support is available to help you feel whole.
>
> *(See a list of internet resources in the back of the book.)*
>
> - Write down the positive ways you've learned to fill your voids
> - Write down any voids you may still need to find healthy ways to satisfy
> - Write down any unhealthy ways you fill voids

SIDEBAR 1

Reading Between the Lines: Exploring Where Our Sense of Self Originates

"Out of that, I created a harmful belief system. I am nothing. I will never amount to anything."

How does someone grow up feeling like, they're nothing and will never amount to anything? That feeling is normal for many victims of childhood abuse or neglect. For some children, these very words were uttered to them by their own parents. Even if you never heard these words, you may have gone through your childhood without being nurtured by anyone. Your early life experiences may have lacked someone who believed in you, connected with you

In the last 50 years, researchers have studied how the nature of the relationships between caregivers and young children, affect the development of secure or insecure attachments. Attachment is both a biological process, involving the development of our 'social brains,' and a psychological process, involving how we think and feel about ourselves. Women that weren't nurtured, believed in, or had healthy emotional connections during childhood; may have lost the mothering instinct.

In fact, what attachment research suggests is that parenting isn't an instinct at all. Parenting is not a biological drive that kicks in when you have a baby. Instead, your early life experiences set you up to either, be able to react in a nurturing way -- or have struggles becoming a nurturing parent. If those early times were marked by abuse or neglect, the very nurturing relationships you crave the most will seem difficult to find. Parenting could actually fill you with dread, anxiety, and frustration.

But here's the good news! Even if you received minimal nurturing or connection during childhood you can become a nurturing parent. To do so requires finding your own nurturing and healthy relationships.

See Sidebar 2 for more on finding healthy relationships.

WHEN MY RELATIONSHIP WITH MOTHERHOOD STARTED TO MATURE

Although I spent the better part of 19 years broke, homeless and living on the streets, I continued having children. Doing so, knowing I was incapable of caring for them properly. Not surprisingly, I lost them. While in prison for my 66th criminal conviction, and pregnant at 37 years old, I was given a chance to keep my last child. I knew things had to be different this time, for my daughter's sake.

I didn't know anything about secure attachments, before my daughter Orlandra was born. Imagine having several other children, not understanding the need for us to have a secure attachment. In the environment where I was raised, no one experienced secure attachments, so they were unable to provide examples of what it looked like. However, I broke that cycle, when I began learning about it through my therapy, *Circle of Security*. This program teaches parents how to pick up on kids' emotional needs, support a child's ability to manage their emotions, help develop children's self-esteem, and fully honor a child's need for true security. I was fascinated by all of it, completely caught up in the bonding process. I decided not to count on Orlandra to fill voids in my life. It was my job to love her unconditionally, not the other way around. I finally realized just how unfair it was depending on my child for my healing, happiness, and safety. Where did I turn to finally find the void-filler, joy-giver, and haven-provider I could depend on? I turned to my newfound relationship with Jesus Christ.

SURVIVING TRAUMA BECAME A PART OF MY RELATIONSHIP WITH ORLANDRA

When I nursed my daughter, it was such an amazing experience. I had never encountered anything like it. The pure joy of looking down at her as she was actually being fed from my body. It was an overwhelming joy I can't begin to describe in words. I didn't want this incredible bond to ever stop. I wanted it to last forever. I thought this was the way, the only way. I was wrong. At the time, I didn't realize my decision making, in regard to my daughter's well-being, was based on my trauma.

An example of this was when staff suggested I supplement Orlandra's breast milk with whole milk. The reason for the suggestion was to make sure Orlandra would receive proper nutrition, if something happened to me. If she wasn't given the opportunity to become accustomed to an alternative to breast feeding, she would not feed well if I wasn't around. It made some sense, but I decided against it. It was my belief, Orlandra would probably refuse anything else after only having breast milk for 15 months. I feared she would let herself go hungry. Since there were so many times I was hungry as a child, I vowed my daughter would never feel the pain and anguish of hunger. Guess what, something happened to me when she was only 15 months old.

On Oct. 31, 2005, I was struck by an SUV while crossing a street in Baltimore City. I woke up in Johns Hopkins Hospital intensive care unit, badly injured and unable to care for my daughter. This meant she had to experience trauma due to our separation, thus breaking our bond. On top of that, now she was forced to take foreign food, doubling her traumatic experience. It was then I realized, my 'just breast milk' decision was based on my past experience, not on what Orlandra really needed from me. I started reading the Bible, praying a lot, and trying to heal. This involved learning how the healing process works and slowly embracing it. However, I was still making bad decisions for us.

ORLANDRA, ME AND MY TRAUMA MAKES THREE

My daughter is 14 years old now. Through the years, I've had to rethink my initial decisions several times. I double check and thoroughly review my decisions, to ensure her well-being. Our current reality is totally different from my past. My triggers are mine, not hers.

Being a single mother was very difficult. It was just us and everything was a mystery to me. I didn't remarry until she was 12 years old. When we moved out of the residential program, I was clueless about running a household. 19 years of homelessness, no place to call my own, how could I understand managing a household on my own. I depended on other people to tell me. I wasn't ashamed about what I didn't know. Instead I was determined to learn, for both our sakes. I had to learn to pay bills and who to pay them to. Learning to not only buy food, but the right food. Buying the right amount of food became a task. There were times when we had too much food, due to my growing up with so little to eat, then becoming homeless. Now I could go to the store and get whatever we needed, and then some.

My abandonment and neglect triggers would hit me while shopping, which should have been happy times. It was especially triggering for me, when the pampers supply was low, food was running out, or there was only one bar of soap left. I would panic and go out and buy too many things. To the point where Orlandra outgrew pamper sizes before they were all gone. I did the same thing with clothes and shoes. Another example, of my trauma creeping into our relationship, was always keeping the refrigerator and all the cabinets fully stocked. Otherwise, I would fear hunger was just outside our door. There could be no open spaces. Even dealing with this I knew, through prayer and trusting God, healing and deliverance were possible.

Then therapy taught me what it really means to be a mother who properly raises, nurtures, and cares for her child. It means making sure Orlandra has what she needs is enough. My old buying habits were unhealthy and unconducive to her well-being. I learned how to maintain a household. Very early on I learned how to create a budget. I kept asking questions, listening to suggestions, and using government assistance.

SIDEBAR 2

Parenting After Trauma

"I knew things had to be different this time. I knew I couldn't count on her to fill that void in my life. My job was to love her unconditionally."

On some level, everyone senses that parenting involves unconditional love. However parents who have never experienced unconditional love, but have suffered trauma, with no healthy interpersonal connections; may struggle with giving unconditional love. If you're someone who knows about trying to fill that void in your life; a person trying to love yourself even when you feel like no one has ever truly loved you, then you know all about how hard it is to parent after trauma.

Recognizing you're stuck is the first thing to do; followed by a scary but necessary step, reaching out for help. Filling the void caused by a lack of connections, is done by creating safe connections. Reaching out to professionals such as; counselors, therapists, or ministers, are probably the best sources for guidance to help establish safe connections.

The path to healing may journey through pain. The truth is, most people that have been abused or neglected don't realize how strong they really are. They can endure the pain of healing. Filling the void within starts by knowing the void exists and being determined to give the people closest to them, what they never received.

See Sidebar 3 for an overview of various parenting interventions that can help with healing.

A NOTE FROM MY DAUGHTER

Mom, I can't even begin to express the amount of gratitude I have for you. You have literally been there for me through my 13 years of existence. As I mature, I have come to realize the importance of having someone special like you to guide me through the good, the bad, and the ugly. I am forever grateful for having you right by my side, no matter what. I really appreciate the times you've stayed up and cuddled with me when I was sick. I will forever act like a baby and need you, even if I only have a cold. Something about your sweet embrace reassures me that I'll be fine again. Then just like that, I feel a thousand times better.

Thank you Mom for being so selfless. I know I'm not the easiest person to please. However I've come to realize, somehow you always find a way to make me happy. You always drop whatever you're doing right away, to come to my rescue, whether it's a ride to basketball or picking me up from a friends' house. I sincerely apologize for all those times I acted ungrateful and spoiled. I now know that you were doing your best, and that's all that matters to me. After what you've been through, I know it's hard to try to fit in sometimes with the other moms at school, but you always try your best to make me feel and look good. Thank you for being my number one support system and being patient with me. You're always my biggest fan. Whether it's basketball games or parties, you're there, no matter what. You try not to miss anything. Now that's what I call dedication!

JOURNAL ASSIGNMENT #3

Have you ever made bad decisions for your child(ren) due to your trauma? If so:

- Write down how it impacted your child(ren)

PRAYER

Heavenly Father, I thank you for the gift of parenthood. Help us to raise our children, to know you, to trust you, and to serve you. Father, may your Holy Spirit guide us always. In the name of our precious Jesus we pray.

Amen.

STARTING A RELATIONSHIP WITH MY ADULT CHILDREN

Reuniting with my adult children has been very difficult. It was incredibly exciting seeking the reunions, but I wasn't prepared for what was to come. I thought it would be 'easy street', forgetting that the word of God says there will be trials and tribulations. Thinking that we could pick up where we left off and trying to be MOMMY to them was way off. My trauma, addiction and homelessness caused my children to be removed from me. When I reunited with two of my sons, they responded to me with resentment and anger, as you might imagine. One son was led to believe lies about me, which added to his anger towards me. There were many times they would say things to me that were hurtful. In defense, I would strike back with my own unkind words. These outbursts always left me feeling cornered and up against the wall. My triggers were all over the place. FIGHT! That was my unhealthy survival mode solution. The reunions definitely didn't go the way I wanted or expected.

I certainly didn't pray enough to prepare me for meeting my sons. Looking back on it, I should have waited until I forgave myself before attempting the reunions. The shame and guilt I carried was overwhelming. Even so, I never stopped thinking about them, never stopped loving them. I always prayed for them. As my relationship with God deepened, I started to really depend on Him to come through with His promise of being a God of restoration. As I got closer to God, the enemy started to work overtime. He used my new-found relationships with my sons and all the things I did in my past to try to make me lose them. It will always be very vivid in my mind. The relationships became toxic, with heated verbal abuse flying back and forth. My sons had a survival mode of their own. It clashed loudly with mine.

THE IMPACT OF THE PAST ON THE RELATIONSHIPS

The definition of a parent; to watch over, to take care of, to raise up, were not part of the relationships I had with my adult kids when we first reunited. We were forming new relationships. Being reminded of our past was very hard for all of us. Not allowing the past to be a part of our relationship caused problems when we talked. At one point, I had to shut the relationships down because they became so abusive. That was painful to do, it felt like I was abandoning them all over again. But I knew in my heart if I didn't take those tough steps to get back together, we would never be able to regroup and move forward. I prayed harder and continued to trust God to be faithful of His promises to me.

I realized we needed therapy. It was impossible with one son, due to his is incarceration. However, my other sons and I did, we recently had our breakthrough. Finally laying all our cards on the table and saying what needed to be said. I realized I had to let my children say what they felt. These honest exchanges were really good times to move toward our reconciliations, though they seemed like anything but good at the time. As a result of candor and hard talks, our relationships are growing to become very tender and loving. In order to achieve and maintain healthy relationships, there were times I had to back up and let them go through whatever they needed to say without saying a word in response. I knew if I didn't, we would go to a place of no return. We would lose any chance of being a family again. They had to forgive me, and I had to forgive myself. This was something that needed to be done as individuals in their own time and at their own pace.

THE BEGINNING OF OUR HEALING FROM THE PAST

I started using my network of folks who could identify with my situation regarding my children. Reaching out for support, suggestions, and guidance from experts and my peers. My relationship with Jesus is how I found my personal forgiveness. If God, the almighty, holy God could forgive me of all of my filthiness and sin, why couldn't I forgive myself? It was the only way for me to truly heal. Forgiveness of yourself and others is necessary for true healing. As I learned to forgive myself, I prayed that God would soften my sons' hearts and allow them to find forgiveness for me. I realized that I had no control over this. I only had control over me and how I coped with all the stressors in my life. I believed God's promises would someday deliver me from shame and guilt. I believed God's promises would somehow deliver my sons from their resentments and anger. I had to understand God in all of this, His plans and His purpose. Only God, our loving and merciful God, could make these changes.

"Trust the Lord with all your heart; lean unto your own understanding, acknowledge Him in all your ways, and He will direct your path."

PROVERBS 3:5

That is the scripture I would hold tightly when dealing with my relationships with my adult kids so one day we can be a family, a loving family, a godly family.

SIDEBAR 3

Finding Security:
How to Be the Parent You Want to Be

Parenting interventions that focus on attachment can offer parents whose lives have been marked by trauma a way to break the cycle.

My story of healing is tied to my daughter Orlandra's story of what it's like to have a mom who puts security first. What does 'putting security first' even mean? Security is a term that comes from research on how babies form attachments to their caregivers. A process that has been intensively studied over the last 50 years. My path to healing included a parenting therapy called *Circle of Security*. Believe it or not, I got that therapy while in a jail diversion program.

The focus of *Circle of Security* is helping people that have experienced insecurity, mistrust, and pain learn about attachment. Identifying the needs of babies and young children as they explore the world, then return to their caregivers for protection or comfort forms attachments. Parents that feel confused or overwhelmed, by the job of caring for a baby, can begin to gain confidence and create secure attachment. Creating security is hard work, but my story proves that it's never too late.

More information on the *Circle of Security* can be found at: https://www.circleofsecurityinternational.com/for-parents.

JOURNAL ASSIGNMENT #4

Did you have secure or insecure attachments with your parent(s)?

Do you have secure or insecure attachments with your child(ren)?

- Write down what you've learned from these relationships that can help you be a better parent

PRAYER

*Father God in Heaven,
give us the strength to make good decisions when it comes to our adult children. Help us to stand firm on your word and your promises, knowing that you love them more than we could ever love them, and that you will guide and protect them always.
In the name of Jesus
we pray.*

Amen.

3

EMPLOYEE

—

*"Lord God, you created heaven and earth
by your great power and outstretched arms;
nothing is too hard for you"*

JEREMIAH 32:17

TRANSITIONING FROM A RECIPIENT TO PROVIDER RELATIONSHIP

Getting a job opportunity after being unemployed, with no real skills most of my life, was amazing to me. I knew it was truly from God. As I started to work in different positions for several companies, I found it wasn't always easy as a trauma survivor. My first job was a dream. I worked for the same trauma-informed care program I graduated from earlier. The staff was already trauma-informed and knew how to work with trauma survivors. So that was a 'no-brainer' for me. I was able to work feeling safe. I had already spent a year around the same people. They knew of my trauma, my triggers, and even some of my tools. I basically moved from receiving services to providing services. It was a great experience. I worked directly with the co-founder of the program. She helped develop in me the ability to trust others. She taught me everything I needed to know as a trauma survivor. She was patient with me and consistent in her approach. I lost the sense of safety I felt while working there, when I moved on to other positions. I began to feel unsafe and insecure. I began experiencing my triggers in the workplace.

TRIGGERS THAT AFFECTED MY WORKPLACE RELATIONSHIPS

I'm always open and transparent about my past. Being an open book caused me to feel misunderstood by some of my co-workers, on many occasions. This honesty led to the development of a fearful paranoia. I spent way too much time thinking about what others thought of me. I wondered, can they see that I've changed? Do they believe I've changed? People would be engaged in idle office talk, not even directed towards me, and I would take the comments personally at times. I would ask myself, "Why would they say such things, when they know about my past?" So, I started doing things to counteract my fears. I would talk loudly and joke about everything, I actually became the office clown, thinking this would divert folks' minds from my past. Instead, it robbed me of my concentration and motivation. I spent more time goofing off than I did being an asset to the team. Thank goodness I realized my need to find tools to use at work to help me stay grounded and self-regulated. Most of my tools that worked at home probably wouldn't do the trick in the workplace. That meant I had to develop workplace tools.

MY TOOLS FOR MAINTAINING HEALTHY WORKPLACE RELATIONSHIPS

For one, I started to work out during my lunch break. In one of my positions, we had access to an on-site gym. That turned out to be a wonderful tool for me. Other times when I was triggered at work, I would grab a cup of tea and take a tea break. Another tool was totally removing myself from everyone. I would shut my office door, put on music, and work alone. My work tools were working! Tea time, music plus solitude. Exercise expanded my toolkit. For the most part people have compassion for trauma survivors, but if they haven't walked in our shoes, they can't truly understand. Therefore, my number one job as a trauma survivor is to deal with my triggers, by making sure I utilize tools to adjust.

You can't hold people accountable for unintentionally triggering you. You can only make them aware. Our triggers are our triggers. Reminding myself that "this is the workplace, not a treatment program", was helpful. I would tell myself, "I need to be accountable for myself and take care of me." I continued to be as transparent as possible, and for the most part, I just need to put tools in my briefcase to cope.

> **JOURNAL ASSIGNMENT #5**
>
> Take a moment and think about a typical day at work, then write your answers to the following questions:
>
> - Do you feel your work environment is safe for a trauma survivor? If so, what makes you feel that way?
> - Do your co-workers know that you're a trauma survivor? If not, do you think it's safe for them to know?
> - Are there things that trigger you at work? If so, what?
> - What are some things you do to help calm you?

- What calms you that you can integrate into your work day. For example, taking a walk to get fresh air or having a cup of tea.
- What are some things you can do to help you feel safe at work? For example, already have music in your office, keep teas at your desk, or identifying someone at work you feel safe to talk to.

4

DATING

—

"I am the Lord your God, who grasps your strong hand, who says to you, don't fear; I will help you"

ISAIAH 41:13

MY NEED FOR DATING RELATIONSHIPS

I wouldn't recommend this, but I started dating while I was still in treatment. My first date was my graduation celebration from the program. I think that was way too soon for me to start dating. Like so many other women, I came out of the treatment program healing from prostitution and everything that goes along with being a drug addict. For us, having someone look at us and give us a compliment, becomes how we determine our worth. A lot of this mindset is due to our history. My daughter was almost six months old when I started to date.

Like most programs treating addictions, we were mandated to go to Narcotics Anonymous. It's funny I use the word 'man-dated' because truthfully, all I ever got out of NA was, a date with a man. I was going to meetings then started repeating unhealthy behaviors, when I started dating. I began looking for validation from someone other than myself, just like I did so many times in my youth. Early in my healing process, the opposite sex was my source for validation. I wanted someone to make me feel good about myself. I was still in the very early stages of forming my relationship with God, what I call a 'baby Christian'. At the time, I was still looking for affirmation from other people. When my Christianity began to bloom, one of the first questions I asked my boyfriend was, "Do you know Jesus?" Once he said yes, that was it! I believed I had my soulmate. I soon realized that saying something and living it are two different things.

MY FIRST RELATIONSHIP

I spent several years with the man that took me on my first date. We met in NA, meaning he was in recovery mode, not necessarily his healing mode. Recovery mode and healing mode are two separate and distinct things. Yes, he was still struggling with maintaining his sobriety and recovery. However, a big plus was that he accepted my daughter as his own and treated her well. We began living together shortly after we started dating. It went against everything I was learning about God and living my life His way. I was still making some unhealthy choices. Because of this and other reasons, I knew the relationship couldn't last. He was aware of my history, but he didn't understand my trauma and certainly not my triggers. In fact, neither did I at the time. I was still in learning mode. How could I tell him all about me if I was still figuring it out? He was never abusive physically or verbally, but it felt like it because he broke my trust through mental abuse. I was unsuccessfully trying to find personal validation through him. Instead, I should have put my trust in God and my own self-worth.

WHAT I WANTED THE RELATIONSHIP TO DO FOR ME

I wanted him to erase all the bad times I had with men from my past. I wanted him to fix all the wrong that was done to me earlier in my life. I wanted him to wipe away all the domestic violence and abuse. I expected him to make everything better for me. But of course he couldn't, how could he. What I was asking of him was more than anyone dating should give. I needed him to accept me as is, and fix everything else. I wanted him to spend all of his time with me. Due to my abandonment and neglect issues, it would trigger me when he didn't. That was extremely unfair of me. Being in recovery, he needed to network to maintain his sobriety. I was asking him to forgo his success by demanding his presence at all times. Requiring him to stop networking with others was literally asking him to give up. Eventually I realized I couldn't monopolize his time. Instead of fixating on him, I should have enjoyed my baby daughter while he networked. I needed to spend time with God, praying for myself and reading the Word.

THE AFTERMATH OF THAT RELATIONSHIP

When that relationship ended, I was still struggling with the whole idea of dating. After our break-up, I didn't want to date at all. It was too hard trying to figure things out for myself to get acquainted with another person's life. For a time I would over analyze situations, thus preventing me from even making it to a second date. I was left feeling alone and damaged until I learned to stop expecting a date to solve all my problems. It's possible to feel safe and secure while developing healthy relationships with the opposite sex. The key is understanding, dating isn't marriage and the man I'm dating is not and will not be my security blanket. When I finally grasped that, I stopped looking for the perfect 'golden boy' in a date. Only Jesus can live up to that expectation. I had to change my way of thinking and add this new awareness to my dating toolkit. I needed to take a look at uncomfortable feelings and stop confusing them with feeling unsafe. Being able to relax, enjoy myself, and know who I was then present that 'me' to the person on the other side was crucial to my healing. I had to realize that everybody I went on a date with wasn't my rapist or my abuser.

MY DATING TOOLKIT

I allowed myself plenty of time to get to know someone. Before a date, I would Google him to feel safe deep within. I would remember to breathe deeply, take it nice and easy, plus listen and learn on dates. I met some good guys and some not so nice guys. As my relationship with God grew deeper and more sincere, I started to look for Christ-like qualities in my dates. I had requirements for whomever I spent my precious time with and chose to date. He would have to understand and relate to me as the Christian woman I was becoming. I wanted to live according to the word of God. Believe me, it helps a great deal when the person you're dating is also living as a Christian. I laid down a blueprint for the man I wanted to spend my time with. I threw out my old way of thinking about what they needed to do for me to feel safe.

I truly believe a relationship should glorify God. I was allowing God to continue transforming me to put forth my best efforts. God was starting to use me and give me a platform for His glory. So in dating it only made sense to consider that as well. Any person I shared my life with would have to understand my obedience to God and His call on my life. By praying and allowing God to lead me, I trusted He would continue to prepare me for the man He was going to send. I started to let go and let God do the dating work for me.

> *"In His kindness, God called you to share in His eternal glory by means of Christ Jesus. So after you have suffered a little while, He will restore, support, and strengthen you, and He will place you on a firm foundation."*
>
> **1 PETER 5:10**

MY FRIEND, NATASHA, TELLS HER DATING STORY

I first heard of Tonier Cain in January 2017 when a friend recommended her documentary, *Healing Neen*. I watched it, marveling at the obvious transformation in this woman's life. "That looks exactly like God," I thought, even though she hadn't mentioned God once in the documentary. I recognized God was there, the one who had also comforted, healed, and changed me, from the inside out. Tonier and I are different, but our God is the same. He is Himself, yesterday, today and forever. While He loves each of us uniquely, just as He made each of us uniquely, He transforms each of us with His same peace, joy, and love when we seek Him. When I came to know Tonier, I quickly realized we had indeed, been sought after and found by the same God.

When Tonier first asked me to share my thoughts on dating after enduring failed relationships, I had no idea where to begin. Would I write about my divorce? Maybe I would write about the many other failed relationships I'd had. I could possibly write about the person I'm dating now, and what it feels like to be in the first healthy relationship of my life. It is often the case that, God's ideas are seemingly contradictory but exactly right. "Of course," I realized. "In a chapter about dating, God wants me to write about being alone."

Being alone has always been my greatest fear. I suspect it comes, at least in part, from not feeling too close with my family growing up. To fill that void, I latched onto relationships. Any man was better than none. Until I was 27, I can't recall one evening in my life I ever spent alone. I wanted so badly to please whomever I was dating.

While I grew up going to church and believing that God existed, it didn't change my day-to-day life. I'd heard plenty of traditional 'Christian' advice for young women. "Rejoice in your singleness," they would say. "Your body is a temple of the Holy Spirit." Yet I found this 'purity talk' ridiculous. "Who would choose to be alone?" I asked. "This talk is just self-righteous and unrealistic." Instead of seeking God when alone, I tried to fill the void by pleasing people.

Oddly, this began a cycle of unhealthy relationships. Under pressure, I had sex at 19 to please a boyfriend who lost interest in me soon after. This pattern continued for years with a variety of boyfriends. One was a Christian whose actions didn't match his words. He advocated for no sex before marriage but, despite my objections, he would take my clothes off and have sex with me. Afterwards, he would lash out at me for causing him to sin! The cycle was exhausting. Yet when I found the courage to end that relationship, I soon began another. Before I knew it, I was 23 years old and married. Rather than living 'happily-ever-after' we entered a dark, terrible downward spiral fueled by alcohol. Three years later I was divorced. Alone once again.

Soon afterwards I fell in love with someone else, someone who seemed to be everything I could possibly want. He appeared to be so different from the men I had dated before. My perfect dream, my idol, but the problem was that my idol was married to someone else. They were separated while getting divorced, and he basically lived with me for over a year. The words on this page cannot begin to express how madly in love and obsessed I became with him. He was my world. He would say, "Please don't ever leave me. I can't live without you. I can't wait to marry you," over and over. His own background was one of abuse and hardship, we became each other's light in a dark place. "He needs me," I thought. He represented all my wildest dreams of a family, and I represented his.

There was a sudden complicating factor. During this 'madly in love' period, I was gripped by the urge to pray. "I haven't thought about God in so many years," I thought. "There's no way He wants to hear from me now", but I started praying anyway. Slowly, gradually, day by day, my relationship with God grew. Now I know, God is Himself. He cannot be anything else. He is love. His love for us is unshakable. No matter what we do, no matter how far we fall, He never leaves us nor forsakes us. By His nature, He cannot. God leaves the 99 to chase the one. God did that for me. Me, the one that did the unthinkable. I'd gotten divorced, lied, cheated, envied, committed adultery and created an idol. All in an attempt to fill my life with something, with someone. To give it meaning through a relationship, a family. Through all of this, the still small voice in my head never faltered. Over and over, as months passed and I pushed it away, it quietly repeated itself. "You have to let him go," the voice said. "Leave everything behind and follow me." Finally I did.

I spent one hot August day sobbing on the floor of my bedroom, begging God for help. The one I loved was gone. We said goodbye because we knew it's what God wanted. "Okay God" I cried, "I give up. I'm done being stubborn. You've broken me. I just want what you want." My heart was shattered into a thousand pieces.

Everything I'd prayed for, worked for, and patiently waited for was gone. All my hopes and dreams for the future were gone. I knew I could never love anyone else. I was a 20-something divorced woman. Every relationship I ever had failed. How did I get here? My sin had overwhelmed me. I couldn't see a way out. My worst fear was happening. I was once more completely and utterly alone, except I wasn't. As I cried my heart out to God that day, something changed. Instead of feeling sorry for myself, I felt sorry to God. It sounds so obvious now, but for the first time, it hit me. I had been worshiping an idol. "I'm so sorry, God," I cried over and over. I made an idol out of a person. Not only this person, but everything he represented that I'd always wanted most of all -- the idea of falling in love, getting married, and having a family. "Will you please forgive me and help me?" I begged. "I'm so sorry." Only God had been there every time a man hurt or wronged me. He was the only one who never failed me. The only one who never would. I constantly pushed Him to the side to chase after the ones who could never satisfy.

I spent the next year entirely alone. I lived by myself, came home from work at night alone. I spent many weekends alone. I suppose this might not be a big deal, for some people. For me, it was previously unfathomable and excruciating at first, but it was necessary. My solitude allowed me to know down to the depths of my soul, what it feels like to experience God's overwhelming love and His inexplicable peace. I wouldn't have learned to hear His still, small, but always persistent voice so clearly. I wouldn't have quietly watched in wonder as He worked to gradually heal, restore, and strengthen me after all the broken relationships in my life. Admittedly, I felt miserable and lonely much of the time. I would come home from an exhausting day at work to my silent empty apartment. Sometimes I broke down in bitter tears. What if nothing ever changes? What if this is my entire life, to always live here alone? My family lives far away. Most of my friends are married with families of their own. Had I messed everything up so badly that it could never be fixed? Had I been forgotten?

God hadn't forgotten me. God loved me too much, in spite of myself, to forget me. God's laws are unbendable. They are tougher than steel. They cannot be broken. There are no shortcuts, no easy paths around them. One of God's laws -- the most important—is to put Him above all else. Above yourself and above everyone else. To love Him most of all. I resisted the idea of 'rejoicing in singleness' years before. I didn't realize this fundamentally requires a deep love of God. By this I mean it is similar to how you deeply love a person. You think of him often, you put him first, you care about him, you want to spend time with him, you tell him your thoughts and listen to his. Just like with a person, this love builds on itself. I found that the more time I spent talking to God, reading his Word, reading others' thoughts about Him in books, and talking with close friends about Him, the more and more I loved Him.

The Bible tells us to love the Lord our God with all our heart, soul, mind and strength. What does this look like in practice? It looks like time, attention, thought, obedience and joy. As John 14:15 says, *"If we love Him, we will obey His commands."* God finally had my obedience, my joyful obedience. I wanted to please him. He finally had my love. As time went on, rather than feeling empty, I began to feel more peace and joy than ever before. My life grew fuller. I trained for and ran a marathon, something I previously never would have ever dreamed of doing. Several months before my divorce, I remember attempting to run one mile and barely finishing, becoming a defeated, frustrated, sweaty mess. Running changed me for the better later on.

At work, instead of watching the clock, I found myself excelling. Rather than dwelling on my own problems, I began serving others through Christian organizations in my community. I developed deep, meaningful friendships with women God brought into my life. My relationship with my family is light years beyond what it has ever been. It's by no means perfect, but at this point it is unrecognizable from what it was before. I sought out my former husband to ask his forgiveness for my many wrongdoings. I was stunned and amazed to find that God had been working on him too. I am now honored to call him my friend. None of these things were accomplished by me alone. God did them when I turned myself over to Him. None of these wonderful changes in my life were derived from conscious decisions on my part. My only 'conscious decision' was seeking God.

Our society views isolation as failure, especially for women. However for many of us, a season of being alone is the only way God can really get through to us. At first, this kind of isolation was so distressing for me. In the end, it turned out to be everything. As always, God knows what is good and what is right long before I do. Good and right things blossom at exactly the right time. They blossom when I'm not even thinking about them, my life has grown so full. Out of the blue God brought someone into my daily life. I am now dating a person who loves God, loves me, and his actions show it every day. Without God's transformative power on me when I was alone with Him, I would not have this relationship. I could not have this relationship. The old me simply was incapable of it. Before God can bless us with His gifts, we have to be capable of receiving them. So often God wants to bless us beyond what we could ever ask or imagine, but He cannot because we are not ready. We don't become the right person by looking for the blessings. We become that person by looking for God Himself.

Matthew 6:33 instructs us to *"Seek first His kingdom and His righteousness, and all these things will be given to you as well."* This isn't a commandment we can simply nod at while we keep pursuing what we want. It is an unalterable law. God waits first for us to seek Him before blessing us. My story is being written, except it's no longer my story alone. It's God's story too. I can't say with certainty who I will marry or if I will ever marry again, even though I'm dating. I can't begin to predict the million unimaginable ways God will show up to surprise and bless me. I can't plan my future and I no longer try. God's ways are better. At times pain and suffering are involved for me to be sure. Other times they involve undeserved blessings beyond comprehension. Sometimes those things are one and the same.

My purpose in sharing my stories is to encourage you to seek Him harder. He is real -- the most real thing there is. More real than any man, any relationship, anything. They are mere shadows compared to His reality. He brings joy, peace, and fulfillment we can find no other way. There is no shortcut. I write this hoping to bring God a small bit of the immense glory He deserves to anyone whose worst fear is loneliness or who feels they have messed up badly, God cannot forgive them. It's for any person hurt by others or who caused hurt to others. I was that person, living with no thought of God. However, in His kindness He restored, supported and strengthened me. All thanks to Him. I live on a firm foundation.

JOURNAL ASSIGNMENT #6

True healing begins within. However, many of us are guilty of trying to find outward solutions to internal struggles. Are you placing that responsibility on the significant other in your life? Have you penalized a significant other for not being able to satisfy your internal needs? Take a moment to make amends in your journal.

- Write a letter taking accountability for unfair expectations you've placed on a significant other
- Write a letter to someone that you've been in a relationship with that placed unfair expectations on you
- Keep the letters and read, revise and add as needed.

PRAYER

My Lord, help us to keep our eyes on you at all times. Let's not go astray. We know that you are with us always and never are we alone. Keep us in your perfect care. We love and thank you. In the name of Jesus.

Amen.

5

MARRIAGE

—

"So then, they are no longer two but one flesh. Therefore, what God has joined together, let not man separate."

MATTHEW 19:6

HOW MY TRAUMA SHAPED MY APPROACH TO MARRIAGE

Marriage by itself is difficult then mix in a traumatic past, it can seem impossible. We're led to believe the beginning of a marriage is supposed to be blissful, beautiful, and exciting, as you embark on a wonderful new journey. What many people aren't told about the journey is that it's going to be work right from the start. When you're a trauma survivor, especially a survivor of sexual abuse and domestic violence, you're faced with more challenges. The least little thing can cause you to be on guard and ready to succumb to old methods of survival, at any given moment. It was never healthy using my old survival modes, fight, flight or freeze. Trauma taught me to protect myself, at any cost. It made me protect myself from the pain and suffering I knew men could inject. It made me feel like I needed to control the marriage. These thoughts mulled around in my mind more and more, activating my survival mode.

My commitment to growth is a daily process. It's impossible to succeed in marriage without working on self and learning how to manage my triggers. The reality is that not all marriages will last. Mine didn't but I'm hopeful for the future. With that said, I thought it was important to include some insight from a couple that is managing to weather the tests of time.

MY FRIEND DESIRAE WRIGHT (A TRAUMA SURVIVOR) ON MARRIAGE

I paused for a moment when Tonier asked me to write about marriage. To say mine has been a roller coaster would be an understatement. The trials and tribulations we've endured over the 20+ years had me thinking I wasn't qualified to write about marriage. However, that's exactly why I am. My husband Chris and I are honored to share what we've learned over the years.

In the beginning, we spent more time fighting over emotional responses to triggers than addressing marital conflicts. Can someone tell me why we're led to believe that the beginning of a marriage is supposed to be this wonderful fairy tale existence? That's not true, and it made us feel like we were doing something wrong. The beginning of our marriage was rough, and the struggle continued for a long time. It takes work for two individuals, with their own traumas and coping mechanisms, to come together and create a new entity - the marriage.

YOURS MINE OURS

You must process the personal before you can improve the marital. It's hard to resolve a problem when you can't differentiate between your personal baggage and marital issues. There have been many instances when we've gotten upset with each other because our perception of an action was blurred by past experiences. Here's an example of how we deposited individual issues into our collective relationship.

Chris liked to buy me just because gifts. For no reason at all he would surprise me. Being thoughtful is a good thing and should be nurtured in a relationship. However, my baggage didn't allow me to view it that way. In my past gifts were given to me in attempts to apologize for or cover up disrespecting me. This led to my defenses going up and becoming suspicious of him every time he did something nice. In turn I never responded the way he wanted, which was triggering for him and led to his defenses going up and building resentment towards me. My trauma prevented me from receiving in the context intended. His trauma prevented him from asking me why. Eventually he stopped and that was triggering. I felt like it was a sign that he didn't care anymore and would leave me soon. The fact that I never asked him why he stopped, made him feel like I didn't notice and took him for granted. Now we've learned how to separate personal (Chris stuff or Desirae stuff) from the collective (the marriage). This is what that same scenario looks like broken down into yours (Chris), mine (Desirae) or ours (the Marriage).

Ours: Showing your spouse that you see them and appreciate them. Anything Chris bought me was an item he remembered I like from previous conversations. That shows he pays attention when we talk and values me by showing me appreciation for no specific reason. Partners should pay attention to the little things and affirm that they're valued in the relationship.

Mine: Feeling unworthy to be loved and that it was unsafe to trust anyone. My trauma caused me to look for reasons to validate being distrustful. It also blinded me from viewing anything as a show of loving affection towards me.

Yours: Personal insecurities feeding a need for praise and internalizing his emotions. His trauma caused him to seek validation of his worth from others. It also caused him to put people into categories that he kept to himself. If you praise me you're for me; if you don't you're against me.

As you can see our marriage suffered because we hadn't dealt with our individual issues. Investing in self care is not selfish. Stepping back and letting your partner deal with their stuff on their own is not abandonment. Putting in the work to repair what you can and release what you can't only makes you stronger when you come together to tackle things as a couple.

COMMUNICATION IS KEY

Sometimes the best communication is articulating that you're not ready to talk. Addressing a situation when emotions are high only makes matters worse. If why you love your spouse is the furthest thing from your mind, it's not a good time to attempt resolving a marital issue. Take the time and space necessary to be able to approach one another in love. I'm the pragmatic partner, so I'm usually ready to delve into working on an issue before Chris. His need to step away was triggering for me because it felt disrespectful. It took time for us to accept how the other needed to cope without taking it personally. Gaining that understanding was key towards leading us into developing healthy communication skills. We had to feel safe for our defensive to come down and began to truly hear and start understanding one another.

SUPPORTIVE COMMUNICATION LEADS TO CONFLICT RESOLUTION

An overview of how to engage in a supportive conversation

Specify what you need

What's required to achieve the following is specific to your individual need:

1. To feel supported
2. To feel respected
3. To feel heard
4. To feel loved

Remain focused on resolution

1. Have conversations not debates
   a. Come together to address potential obstacle for maintaining a healthy partnership
   b. Let go of pointing fingers and what you dislike, focus on what's needed to move forward
   c. Hear what your spouse is saying as THEIR TRUTH instead of an attack on you
   d. Share what you can do to help overcome the obstacle
   e. End with an action plan

Be mindful of your partners triggers

1. Actively provide your spouse with what they need to feel supported during the conversation
2. Remain open and receptive despite your emotional response to what you're hearing

Be honest

1. Verbally share your feelings that arise during the conversation, in a calm respectful manner
2. Step away from the conversation if it becomes too emotionally overwhelming or too difficult to continue in a respectful and supportive way
3. Set a time to resume the conversation if a break is needed

ALLOWING GOD INTO MY MARRIAGE

If you drink too much, fall and crack your tooth, do you expect God to take that chip away? It's up to you to make the appointment, go to the dentist and pay the price, if you want to fix what you damaged. Marriage works the same way. I was going to church expecting God to fix what I broke. There was no way of getting around having to do the hard, painful work of healing old wounds to move forward. The blessing is, when you allow God into your marriage, He provides you a road map to navigate over the tough terrain. My problem was that I didn't know how to tap into His guidance, especially when triggered. Eventually I learned how to hear and follow, but it was a process.

My first step was asking God to ease my pain instead of taking matters into my own hands. As soon as I'm triggered, I start talking to God. Not in a fancy eloquent prayer, but raw emotion driven pleas for help. I ask for help not to do what my emotions are pushing me towards. Lord knows He kept me from catching a case on more than one occasion. I ask for Help to overcome the weight and darkness of what I'm feeling. Help to understand how I ended up in my situation and how to keep from ending up here again. My talks with God aren't always calm. Speaking from a place of emotion means it's going to come out however it needs to at that time. I yell, cry, and even scream if necessary. It's what I call 'my emotional purge'. A feeling of relief follows every purge. I'm always in a better place mentally after emotionally talking to God. I move from being fueled by emotion to resting in peace. That peace allows me to be still. In the stillness is where I receive direction. Being still is challenging for me which requires the focus of my conversations with God to shift. Now my prayers switch from emotional outcries to affirmations of faith, based on the Word of God.

> *So shall my word be that goeth forth out of my mouth: it shall not return unto me void, but it shall accomplish that which I please, and it shall prosper in the thing whereto I sent it.*
> **ISAIAH 55:11 (KING JAMES VERSION)**

I believe God's word will not return void, so I speak His word for strength to persevere. His reassurance helps me to remain still until God reveals His next steps for me. I don't mean stop moving completely, just being patient and wait for God to reveal himself. I still go about taking care of the day to day and living my life. The difference is that I'm comforted knowing I'm not doing it on my own. God is with me and will guide me along the way. It's during these times of submission that I'm in tune with His direction. Then, when I know the direction comes from God I follow, whether it feels good or makes sense to me. This process is how I transitioned from making a mess of my marriage to learning how to nurture it. It's a continuous process. I don't always get it right, but His grace and mercy is with me and you. No matter how far of course we go, God's love is with us every step of the way. He will always lead us in the right direction, if we trust and believe in Him.

JOURNAL ASSIGNMENT #7

Although marriage is a partnership it's important to hold on to your individuality to maintain a strong union. A well-balanced individual makes for a great partner, which establishes a firm foundation to build a healthy relationship.

- Write down the ways you pay attention to your own triggers
- Write down the ways you pay attention to spouse's triggers
- Write down the ways you pay attention to your marital needs
- Has it been hard for you to be intimate with your spouse?

PRAYER

Father in Heaven, give us patience as you are patient with us, help us to love tenderly and gentle as you do us, help us to be forgiving as you forgive us, help us to be one in marriage and enjoy the fruits. In the sweet name of Jesus.

Amen.

6

FRIENDSHIP

—

"A man who has friends must himself be friendly, but there is a friend who sticks closer than a brother."

PROVERBS 18:24

OBSTACLES TO ESTABLISHING FRIENDSHIPS WHILE HEALING

Establishing friendships were very difficult for me in the beginning of my healing process. Even after God delivered me, being around a lot of different people and learning how to develop healthy friendships was challenging. Honestly, it was something I didn't want to do because I didn't consider myself good friendship material. Number one, I didn't know how to be a good friend. Number two, I didn't think it was necessary. It's hard for me to sit around with people and have every-day conservations about the day or the weather. Small talk like that all seemed useless. My specific problem was that I always checked out in my mind if others were watching and judging me. If I felt like I was somehow being evaluated during a conversation, I wouldn't invest in getting to know the person. Instead of really listening and responding to what others were saying, I would always nod and laugh when they laughed so it seemed as if I were present. In reality, I wasn't most of the time. This was the same defense mechanism I used when I was being abused.

It worked well enough then, but it was a hindrance for developing healthy adult relationships. I think back to my Narcotics Anonymous days. Even in the meetings where everybody had common issues and problems, it was very hard for me to network. I would go in letting my mind wander, analyzing and judging people due to my very unpleasant past. I wondered about the unkind things on their minds. Did they think I wasn't good enough for them? Those thoughts tumbled through my mind. Of course, it was totally unfair and certainly not Godly. I had so many trust issues, it was better for me to see potential deceptions before getting to know these people and letting them into my life. There were times in the beginning of my friendships I wouldn't tell the truth or give real, honest opinions and good feedback. Instead I'd say things to please them or make them feel good. I came to realize this was not being a true friend. In fairness to me, after my horrid past, it's only natural to have the mentality that everyone was out to get me or get something out of me. There have been times when I was burned by so-called friends after starting to finally develop friendships. I even found it difficult to fellowship in church, during the beginning of my healing process. The only time I would get excited about getting together was when I could talk about Jesus. I love talking about Jesus! I wasn't ready to make myself available for other conversations.

WHAT IT TOOK FOR ME TO BUILD HEALTHY ADULT FRIENDSHIPS

Trauma survivors engage in social interaction at their own pace. It's important for survivors, even trauma experts like me to make an effort to make friends quickly. Socializing is a key part of the healing process that moves you towards a better place. Learning about and meeting new people from different races and cultures was exciting to me. My enthusiasm about the new experiences helped me open up. I learned to be more open to friendships which are such important relationships. It wasn't all rosy.

I had to forgive others for what they did to me. Forgiving and trusting has been a long process. Changing my negative behavior toward others was necessary because it prevented me from developing healthy adult friendships. I had to stop thinking people needed to act a certain way or treat me a certain way, before they could be my friend. I had to stop requiring people to be extra special in order to be close to me. They had to be the total opposite of people that hurt me in my past. Of course, this was an impossible expectation and very unfair to people I met. A couple of people I thought were friends hurt me, but I was blessed more than I was burned. I had to learn how to trust myself in being a friend besides learning to trust others. I had to trust myself to be truthful as a friend. I wanted to be a good friend because I had good friends. They deserved the very best I could be in return.

WHAT TRUE FRIENDSHIP LOOKS LIKE

God started to surround me with people who were sincere, caring, good folks. When I called they listened to me and gave me really good advice, whether I wanted to hear it or not. I needed to learn how to respond the same way when my new friends would reach out to me. It is said the only way to have good friendships is to be a good friend. My journey of learning to be a friend has been richly rewarding. I have wonderful friendships today. Some of them are Christians, others are not. I have friends that are Democrats, Republicans, and some who don't care for either party. I have tons of wonderful people surrounding me now.

I want to be obedient to God. When I think about friendship, the scripture that comes to mind is the second greatest commandment, *"Love thy neighbor."* The only commandment greater than this is *"Love thy God, with all your heart."* I truly believe it is impossible to keep the first without keeping the second. I want to love honestly and love with a pure heart. I want to be a friend not of convenience but of conviction. Accepting people for who they are and meeting them where they are is a great beginning to becoming a good friend. I continue to pray for a spirit of discernment, and I ask God to lead me and give me a heart for others through prayer. I can now allow myself to be an honest and present friend, a good friend.

> **JOURNAL ASSIGNMENT #8**
>
> Ask yourself, does what I see in people block me from getting close to them, or is it what I'm afraid they will see in me. Maybe it's a combination. Don't let your fears prevent you from experiencing the support and love of a true friend.
>
> - Write down what causes you to distrust others
> - Write down what you're afraid of others knowing about you
> - Write about a time you haven't been a good friend

PRAYER

Father God, help us to help one another. The second greatest commandment is to "Love thy Neighbor." Show us how, Father, that we can be made pleasing in your sight and a blessing to others. In the name of your precious Son Jesus, we pray.

Amen.

7

BUSINESS OWNER

—

*"Commit your work to the Lord,
and your plans will succeed."*

PROVERBS 16:3

MY CHILDHOOD DIDN'T NURTURE AN ENTREPRENEURIAL SPIRIT

At age 9, I wasn't thinking about what I would grow up to be. I wasn't thinking and dreaming about who I would become. I was thinking about that man who pulled me closed to him as he touched me. As a sexually assaulted child and a child of neglect and abandonment, I couldn't get past any of those things to dream DREAMS.

My childhood created my belief system. I grew up poor in a home run by a damaged, traumatized single mom. I am the oldest of 10 children. Our home wasn't a nurturing household, actually it was the total opposite. Positive affirmations weren't being spoken over my life although I wanted my spirit and soul to be fed. I wasn't being told that I was smart and could accomplish anything. Born into a completely dysfunctional family, I developed the belief that I was nothing. I believed I could never amount to anything. The way things were was just how it was going to be for me. You don't have dreams, goals, or aspirations when you have that kind of belief system.

HOW MY TRAUMA CAUSED ME TO DOUBT MY ABILITY TO OWN A BUSINESS

I refused to even try and achieve what God called me to do. I felt unable to fulfill my purpose that God pre-destined for me long ago. My traumatic past would rise up to try and hold me hostage. Dealing with years and layers of trauma affected my ability to shift to a positive belief system. Brutal sexual assaults, domestic violence, 19 years of homelessness, my lost children, prostitution, being told I was mentally ill, and multiple incarcerations, caused me to believe I was unable to do something amazing like starting my own business.

I struggled as an employee, so how could I be an employer? It was easy for me to get a job, but because of my past trauma, maintaining it was my challenge. My triggers would come in all forms, smells, and colors, which was problematic in the workplace. My difficulties caused me to realize, I needed to own my own business. Working for myself would minimize my occurrences of being triggered. This is not to say that the triggers stopped when I set up my own company; but the change gave me more ways to overcome them when they hit. I was still reminded of my weaknesses and things I did in my past. These traumatic reminders certainly could have prevented me from taking that faith walk and starting my own business.

WHY BEING AN ENTREPRENEUR IS RIGHT FOR ME

To even consider becoming a business owner, I had to overcome my 'can't do' belief system and change my negative thought process. Then and only then was I able to begin to believe I could do something as amazing as owning my own business. Being an entrepreneur afforded me the freedom to remove myself when triggered, without any possible consequences, and set my own tone and pace. Owning my business gave me the luxury of flexibility and control over my environment. Control is important because I need it over my schedule, my time, and picking and choosing who I worked with and when. There were certainly some cons, but the balance scale tipped more to the pros side. It was also a huge walk of faith that was well worth it. Earlier in life my decision was to make a living by having really good jobs and government benefits. However, after five years of that I wanted independence by starting my own consulting business, and it worked out well.

God has been so faithful, even during that pivotal point in my life. I took the plunge, and today I'm CEO of not one, but four companies. There are still times I'm reminded of my past, and that old 'stinking thinking' tries to creep back into my mind. When it happens, I pull out a tool from my toolkit. The basic tools I use are looking at my new life and how far I've come. I remind myself to stay in the present. My professional independence helps me live a better life.

I've been clean and sober for years now. I'm doing a pretty good job at raising my daughter, if I do say so myself. I have great friends, and I have God. All these tools counteracts negativity and weakness with positivity and strength, empowering me as a business owner. We all have strengths, and positive attributes. If you're reading this book, you're doing something positive. This maybe something you wouldn't have done before. Just taking this step is a big plus.

THE BENEFITS OF FAITH IN BUSINESS

Despite my rough background and lack of any real education, much less higher education, I was truly blessed to get the two jobs I landed. Having no real job skills, or training of any kind, I worked for a pair of really great organizations. God placed me in a position where interviews were easy. During the interviewing process I was told they wanted to hire me, so I was never nervous. How blessed for me! While seeking employment, I had a lot of things going for me and few against. This is quite unusual for most people coming out of corrections and addiction.

You know the great thing about walking in faith? When you do, you will walk in obedience, and God will honor it with victories. What others and I could not see, He did. My belief system told me my accomplishments would be impossible, society confirmed that view. Society couldn't see past my addiction, mental illness, incarcerations, homelessness, and prostitution. However, thanks to God's mercy and grace, I did and my belief system changed. All that seemed impossible became my reality. I am living the best possible life now, so I continue to trust God and believe. The Bible says, *"For with God nothing shall be impossible."* Luke 1:37

JOURNAL ASSIGNMENT #9

We all know people who've let their past limit their expectations for their future. Have you allowed fear to block your success?

- Write down what you have yet to accomplish in life

- Write down obstacles you've faced reaching your goal(s)
- Write down your abilities that support reaching your goal(s)

PRAYER

*Our Father in heaven,
your word says, whatever we pray
for in faith and believe, it will be, please
help us to always remember your word,
your promises and your faithfulness,
for we know all things are possible with
you. Thank you, Our Lord.
Thank you. In the name
of Jesus we pray.*

Amen.

8

CHILD OF GOD

—

*"But those who did welcome him,
those who believed in his name, he authorized
to become God's children."*

JOHN 1:12

I'VE HAD SO MANY STAGES IN MY LIFE SEEKING GOD

I wasn't introduced to God as a child living with my mother. We didn't go to church. The time I spent in foster care with my cousin introduced me to the Lord. I always knew there was a God, we had to come from something, but I didn't learn about Him with my mother. Leaving my cousins home and going back to my mother meant the end of church for me. I reverted back to the unseemly life I had before staying with my cousin. At age 14 I attempted suicide. Afterwards I went to live with my aunt and uncle for a time. They didn't attend church, so I still wasn't any closer to getting to know God.

Earlier, I mentioned living with my cousin and being introduced to God. She would send us to church every Sunday, but I still didn't understand who God or Jesus was. I heard people say the Lord's prayer. I didn't know it, so I'd bow my head and murmur a few of the words or say nothing. I was actually baptized at age 12 because my cousin said, "You have to get baptized in the church I attend."

As an adult my good friends Kathy and Kenney would take me into their home. They taught me more about God. I started to see God differently through them because they so lovingly embraced me. They even sent me to a Christian program out of state, but I still wasn't developing a personal relationship with God. I didn't know how. In the program we were told to read the bible most of the day, but I wasn't gaining understanding. At this point, I still didn't understand who Jesus was. It's very hard to begin to have a relationship with a holy God without knowing who Jesus is.

MY MISCONCEPTION OF GOD

Interestingly enough, the man eight years my senior, that I met and married as a teenager, actually attended church every Sunday. Before we were married I would go with him to church, then sneak around with him at his mother's house. He was living two different lives; one as a church-going man and one who did as he pleased. I started to see God, not so much as a holy God as I know him to be now, but as a God allowing people to go to church on Sundays to worship Him, but then turn around and lead un-Godly lives the other six days of the week.

My then-husband would take me to church, sing in the men's choir and serve on the altar. Then we would drink and he would become abusive. I didn't have an opportunity then to see God as a loving God, certainly not as a savior. I wasn't learning the truth about Jesus. All I could see was that you went to church, sang the hymns, and listened to the pastor. Then you went home to be an alcoholic, abused, or abusive. Clearly, this didn't give me a good understanding of who God is.

I BEGAN TO SEE THE TRUE GOD

After that husband left me, my oldest son was taken away, 19 years as a homeless crack-addict and prostitute on the street, shuffling in and out of prison; I began to see the true God. How did it happen, since there weren't a lot of people on the streets talking about God? I was learning a little bit more about Him in prison by attending some church services. Honestly, I went to get out of my cell, but I started asking God to help me more. He was now my Heavenly Father, but what does this Father's love feel like and look like? I didn't know because I had not had that experience. My human father left very early in my life. I needed God to help me to understand, even then, what a fathers' or Fathers' love is. I received Jesus Christ as my Lord and Savior. I knew that I am now a child of God and He's my heavenly Father. I had to pray to God to clearly reveal that me, He did.

MY RELATIONSHIP WITH GOD GREW FROM BITS AND PIECES

I spent 19 years going in and out of prison with only bits and pieces of awareness about who God is. I looked at other faiths and I didn't understand them either. They just didn't seem right to me, so I went back to the Christian faith. Even though I didn't know anything about Catholics I learned how to pray the rosary. I was just trying to pray and do all I could to get out of prison. Whatever prayer I thought might work at any given time, that's what I did. It became a mere convenience for me. However, I would leave God there when the prison gates opened and I was released. I would never take Him back to the streets with me, and I went right back to my old ways. Everything I learned about God was gone just like that. Going back to that instant gratification of crack cocaine, alcohol and street life, was a more immediate answer for me. I no longer needed to wait on God. I was going to go out there and fix myself with whatever I could get my hands on. Of course, I would go back and forth to prison because the bad old ways got me the same old results. I went back to darkness, and I was OK with that. I became very content with my yo-yo life. My relationship with God during that time was pretty minimal. I never took it seriously. I didn't become sincere until 15 years ago.

I was in prison and pregnant again. Suddenly, I felt something in my spirit say, "Since all else has failed, why not look up to God?" I laid on the concrete floor in my prison cell, curled up in the fetal position. For the first time I cried desperately and sincerely to God for help. I cried out for hours, "Please help ME!" I began to truly seek God with all my heart. My search included reading the word of God and praying sincerely. I started to apply the Word of God so I could feel his presence in my life. That's when my heart started to change. I asked Him to forgive me. I also read the Gospel so I could learn who Jesus truly is. I learned that He gave his life for me, and that He loves me so much he laid his life down for me. When I fully understood who Jesus was, I also understood I could indeed be a child of God. I now wanted to please God, I wanted to feel like His child.

GOD WAS THE ONLY THING THAT SEEMED TO WORK

It wasn't all roses the moment I got up off that concrete floor in my prison cell. I had many stages to go through, many challenges to meet, and many set-backs to endure in my walk with Christ Jesus. In relationships when I had sex outside of marriage, I would cry afterward because I knew it wasn't pleasing to God. I was having hook-ups with guys all over the country because I didn't want to let anyone get too close to my heart, thus being able to hurt me after the relationship failed. I ended up letting someone in, we dated 18 months. The year we broke up, he committed suicide a week before my birthday. I really didn't know what to do, so I did the only thing I knew. The only thing that seemed to work, cry out to God.

I prayed more and started to seek God more. I stopped hooking up or seeing anyone. To get sexual release, I watched porn and masturbated. However, that felt even worse than hooking up with men. All of this was going on as I was in a relationship with God. I thanked God for his spirit of conviction. Since nothing I did felt right, I just prayed harder and cried out to Him louder. I would roll on the floor shouting out, "God I know this is not pleasing to you. Please help me!" My prayer life became deeper, and I started abstaining from everything. I had to believe in His word, that He would somehow provide all my needs. This way I was able to stay in my relationship with God. I allowed God to show me who I am in Him and who He is in me. I didn't give up on God, because he didn't give up on me.

The wonderful thing about God is he knows all. He knows our weaknesses. He knows where we struggle with our flesh and how we fail in other ways. That's why he gave us his only begotten son, Jesus Christ, who shed his blood to wash away all our sins. He will erase all our sins from his memory and throw them into the sea of forgetfulness. He knows as long as we live in these bodies of flesh, we will struggle with our sins. We can overcome through prayer and reading the Word of God. We will be strengthened. Being a child of God is fully relying on His grace, mercy, provision and love.

If we truly and fully submit to God's will, He will bring us to a place where He begins to transform our hearts and minds. Then, we will fully activate His spirit that He gave us after His resurrection and ascension. We will sit at the right hand of the Father. We will truly understand His great powers, His plans, and His purpose for our lives as we walk in obedience. Jesus fought and won the battle. Now, we walk victoriously as a Child of God! Glory! Glory to God!

I was so thrilled that my sister LaTonya wanted to share her story and her journey with God.

MY SISTER, LATONYA EDWARDS, CHILD OF GOD

My name is Latonya Edwards. I'm a wife and a mother of two boys. I've had a childhood full of pain and confusion. My mother was beaten by her husband and lost two children before I was born. Her childhood trauma left her numb. By the time my siblings and I came along, we got only what little was left of her. She had no support and I used to watch her cry a lot and drink to make her pain go away. My father, may he rest in peace, was an alcoholic when I was growing up. After years of alcoholism, he got sick. He was there, but not there. I'm sure you know what I mean.

I struggled in elementary school, not because I had learning disabilities, but because I always worried about adult issues as far back as third grade. At the time I thought I was dumb because I couldn't focus on my school work. This mentality followed me in school until I dropped out in ninth grade. I just gave up since I had no support. With my mother being unstable, I began to spiral out of control, running away and being at places I shouldn't have been. Dropping out of school was one of my biggest losses. The second one was losing my virginity. I didn't realize it when I allowed the son of my mother's friend to take that from me at the age of 12.

That was the beginning of my self hate. The person I let do this to me was a hateful person. I watched him hurt my mother verbally and physically, all because we had to stay in his house. I was really afraid of him. One night as I was sleeping in his sister's room, he came in and got me. There were no adults in the house, just other children/teens having sex. He got me out of bed and told me to come with him. He put me in his bed in another room which was a mattress on the floor. He was a big and scary boy, so I didn't say stop, no, or anything at all. I knew how angry he could get and just submitted. There was so much pain from his weight on me. Yet, I said nothing. I hated myself for not stopping him. After that, lacking love for myself and getting none from my parents, I just didn't have anything to give anybody. I thought it was all my fault. I dealt with self- hatred by allowing myself to be abused by a man five years older than I was. Fourteen at the time and staying in a crack house, I thought because he bought me things, he loved me. Not so, that bought my self-esteem down even lower. I started to drink and smoke weed to get away from my pain. I hated having sex because it reminded me of how I lost my virginity. My response was to get high, drink, and sleep around. I didn't have any other examples to follow.

The most hope I had for myself was that I might clean somebody's hotel room and live in public housing. I just couldn't see anything else in my future. I had become everything I didn't want to be, but then came GOD! After being in the streets where I learned how to sell drugs, fight, and live recklessly, I began to sense God was with me. Otherwise, why didn't I get into a lot more trouble than I did?

Sure, I had a couple of run-ins with the law, but nothing heavy. I can say today God had a plan for me, though I didn't see it then. I was constantly giving myself to the entire world in every way. You want something from me? Take it, I was so empty and lost. I even thought about killing myself a number of times. Seeing who I had become was making it so hard to live with myself. I knew God existed, but I just didn't know what that meant for me. I needed to be loved and someone to love, so I tried to get pregnant for years thinking it was the answer. It wouldn't happen. I can thank God for that today!

At age 19, while living with one of my sisters and her two kids, I filled out an application for public housing. I was approved for myself and my little sister, who had a baby girl of her own. We were living in the 'hood,' but at least we had a roof over our heads and were grateful for that. I felt like I had accomplished one big dream, which was to have a place to call my own. I couldn't see anything more than that. Though a child, I felt like an adult dealing with adult issues. For example, as a child we were often getting evicted or being put out of someone's home but there was God, all the while. I started to work at fast food places and hotels so I could care for myself. I wondered who would hire a high school dropout to do anything else. So I never tried. I would still go out and party, drink, and smoke. When I sat down and started to think, all I had were negative thoughts about myself. I thought the partying, drinking and smoking kept me happy and away from my problems. If only I had been right.

On another note, I believed I'd messed my body up because I couldn't get pregnant. This made me wonder, "What am I here on earth for?" I thought only a baby could validate me. I was also so lonely. In 2002, I started dating my husband. He was 17 at the time and already had a new baby of his own. We had known each other a long time. I used to stay with one of his family members and the abusive ex-boyfriend I had. My now-husband knew my background, so we gave it a try. What was so different about him? He never tried to have sex with me after I told him I was tired of sex. He respected that and waited until I was ready. We dated and struggled with being in a relationship. We were both young and knew nothing about love. In 2004, I became pregnant with my first son, Brandon Jr. I was 23 years old. For the first time, I was excited about life. I knew it was God! Life finally had meaning. I was able to stop drinking and smoking and have a heathy baby. Mentally, I was still a mess and my attitude toward life changed back to a feeling of hopelessness.

I had this brand-new baby boy, but no education and still living in the hood. It came down on me like a ton of bricks. I watched so many young boys' lives get lost to the streets. With all the negative self-talk, it seemed to say, "What can you possibly do but destroy this kid's life?" I'm looking at my tender baby boy sleeping. I cried out, "GOD PLEASE HELP ME!" I was desperate. I remember struggling and I didn't want hopelessness and despair for him. Time went on. I worked hard to support my baby. I gave him everything I could working for $10 an hour. I tell you all this because God is never deaf to out cries, no matter how dismal things seem. Psalm 55:17 says, *"Morning, noon, and night I cry out in my distress, and the Lord hears my voice"*. He knows your pain, but we have to know He cares and will help us.

In 2009 I had another boy and named him Chance. We were still together trying to be a family. We had no idea how we were doing it. I had become homeless with my two boys. I made some wrong choices, leaving me without my own home. Can you imagine? All my childhood memories came back, and here I am, taking my kids through the same thing. I needed God more than ever, not just to give me a place to live, but to help me mentally, as well. For so many years I was fighting not to become an alcoholic because that was my parents' hiding place. I would take care of my kids during the day and drink at night. It was so painful to know I failed my kids, but drinking wasn't my worst problem, self-hate was. Then God began to give me a hunger for Him, just when I was so tired of being hopeless. I needed a real change in my life. Acts 10:34 says, *"Then Peter opened his mouth and spoke of a truth I perceived, that God is no respecter of persons."* I've seen people lives changed.

During the time I was homeless between 2008 and 2010, staying here and there but couldn't get stable, I accepted an invite from my oldest sister Tonier. She welcomed me and my two sons in to her home, and she treated us so good. I was finally able to rest my mind. The hunger God gave me was still there, and with that peace, I was able to seek him. I began to ask my sister questions about God and the Bible. I just knew whatever I was doing on my own just wasn't working. I needed change within me. My sister would so graciously come into my room every night and answer any questions she could. She told me to pray about any other questions she couldn't answer. She would also tell me about her favorite Bible stories and how they helped her. My faith began to grow. She gave me a beautiful bible that was given to her and she told me to never stop reading it. In that down time in my life, I was able to look up to God. I just wanted to know who He was. Well, God blessed me with another apartment in public housing for me and my boys! I was so grateful.

I still tried to party my pain away, but it seemed to stop working. I no longer felt good doing it. I actually felt worse. My kids father and I weren't getting along. It seemed every relationship in my life was nonexistent. My heart turned back to God. I think there is only one God, and His name is Jesus. God showed me who He was when He led me to read the Book of John. John 1:1 says, *"In the beginning was the Word, and the Word was with God, and the Word was God."* John 1:14 says, *"And the Word was made flesh, and dwelt among us, and we beheld His glory, the glory as of the only begotten of the Father, full of grace and truth."* I didn't belong to any church, but I felt in my heart that I had to go somewhere and worship.

God is so amazing. He sent his followers out one summer afternoon. While sitting outside with two of my sisters. a man named Tony and a young lady named Noelle came and witnessed to us. They shared God's word with us and what it said about Salvation. They read Acts 2:38 , reading *"Then Peter said unto them, repent and be baptized in the name of Jesus Christ for the remission of sins, and ye shall receive the gift of the Holy Ghost."* My heart was so ready, I asked if I could get baptized right away. They took me, and I repented of my sins and received Jesus as my Lord and Savior. I received the gift of the Holy Ghost a month or so later and spoke in tongues just as the apostles did. Acts 2:2-4 reads, *"And suddenly there came a sound from heaven as of a rushing mighty wind, and it filled all the house where they were sitting. And there appeared unto them cloven tongues like as of fire, and it sat upon each of them. And they were all filled with the Holy Ghost, and began to speak with other tongues, as the spirit gave them utterance."* I can say it was so powerful! God wasn't only with me but He now lived in me! It's been almost seven years since I said yes to Jesus.

I have to be honest. I thought my life was going to be easy in the beginning because I thought all the pain and sorrow I've been through in life had to get better. God did start moving on my behalf quickly. He placed some people of God into my life who did nothing but feed me love. When I would stumble, they would be right there to help me up every time. I had never felt anything like it before. I knew it was real because I wanted to change due to Gods desire living in me. Yet, I still struggle. I struggled before, and I struggle now. I still have some healing that needs to take place. I know God will go deep into my heart and heal. He will get rid of the shame, guilt, sorrow and insecurity. Only God can do that, no human being. Jeremiah 30:17 reads, *"For I will restore health unto thee, and I will heal thee of thy wounds, says the Lord."* I struggle with sin for sure! I don't like to look at myself in the mirror at times because I still struggle with loving myself, but God is always with me. His Word promised to never leave or forsake me. Consider Deuteronomy 31:6: *"Be strong and of a good courage, fear not, nor be afraid of them, for the Lord thy God, He it is that doth go with thee. He will not fail thee, nor forsake thee."*

At times I forget that. I can't tell you how many times I wanted to give up. I can't give up since God has bought me so far. Being a child of God gives me the right to cry out to Him for any and everything. You see how your kids cry out to you when they're hurt or even when they make a mistake? My God! Our love comes from Jesus to give to our children. So His Love is way greater than mine, and He forgives and forgets. In 2012 Brandon and I got married. After being together 10 years with two kids, something had to give. Most of all, I wanted to please God with how I lived my life. It's been about seven years we've been married. Let me tell you God wasn't always pleased with me. I tried so hard to change my husband. I was hurting him. Jesus gave me so much love, I wanted my husband to have it too, but that wasn't my job to do. I had to get out the way and love him as Jesus loves me. God has been working on Brandon and me. We are in a much better place than we were a year ago. We haven't given up on each other. Thanks be to God!

I have to share motherhood with you. It's been rewarding and scary at the same time. I have a good idea how my boys would turn out if it weren't for Jesus. It would not be a happy place. My sons are my everything. Once I became a mom, to me it meant giving them everything I never had. I never left my boys' side. But most importantly, I can give them Jesus and I do. Heaven knows, I'm not perfect at being a mom I'm still trying to find balance in it all with the help of Jesus. Yet, as you know, I had a hard time in school and just gave up. I find myself being extra hard on my boys because it scares me to think I might fail them in this area. I have to pray for help because they don't yet understand, but they will. Jesus is so good He gave me the desire to go back to school and get my high school diploma. I did it while working full-time. That was God at work! I didn't have to tell about the importance of school. I showed them by going back myself. God told me to model the best way I can and I did, with his help. It felt amazing. I'm not who I thought I was. Praise God! For a child growing up feeling like no one cared about her, I've come a long way. I'm now a coordinator/caregiver for a retired dentist. She has entrusted me with her life. I love my job, and there can be no doubt I'm where He's placed me. Jesus reminds me that I have everything I need inside of me. I get down at times. Then, Jesus helps me get my mind right by focusing on Him. My walk with God is just like a roller coaster. The seatbelt is God's protection, the twist and turns are my daily walk. The ups and downs are my mountains and my valleys. The highs and lows are my fears and uncertainties.

Getting to the end is my faith. Here is Ephesians 6:13-17: *"Wherefore take unto you the whole armor of God, that ye May be able to withstand in the evil day, and have done all, to stand. Stand therefore, having your loins girt about with truth, and having on the breastplate of righteousness; and your feet shod with the preparation of the gospel of peace. Above all, taking the shield of faith, wherewith ye shall be able to quench all the fiery darts of the wicked. And take the helmet of salvation, and the sword of the spirit, which is the Word of God."* I've shared my walk. It's not perfect but all so worth it. God has never left my side. Don't give up. There's nothing too hard for God! Matthew 19:26: *"But Jesus beheld them, and said unto them, 'With men this is impossible, but with God all things are possible.'"*

JOURNAL ASSIGNMENT #10

Now that you've finished the book, write a letter to yourself reminding you of the important points you want to remember

- Do you plan on applying anything from the book, if so what?

- Has the book helped you let go of anything in your life, if so what?
- Has the book provided you tools to improve your relationships, if so what?
- Include anything else you found empowering and helpful to you moving forward

PRAYER

*Our Heavenly Father,
we thank you and we are eternally grateful for the blood of your son Jesus that has washed away our sins, so we now are called your children. In the powerful name of Jesus, we pray.*

Amen.

APPENDIX

PREVALENCE OF TRAUMA

- Fifty-six percent of general adult population samples reported at least one traumatic event. (Kessler et al., 1995)

- Ninety percent of mental health clients have been exposed to a traumatic event, and most have multiple experiences of trauma. (Muesar, 1998)

- Three-quarters of women and men in substance abuse treatment report abuse and trauma histories. (SAMHSA/CSAT, 2000)

- Ninety-seven percent of homeless women with mental illness experienced severe physical and/or sexual abuse, 87 percent having experienced this abuse as both children and adults. (Goodman, Dutton et al., 1997)

- Of incarcerated girls, 92 percent reported sexual, physical, or severe emotional abuse in childhood. (Acoca & Dedel, 1998)

- Being abused or neglected as a child increases the likelihood of arrest as a juvenile by 59 percent. (Widom, 1995)

- Three million children are suspected of being victims of abuse and neglect. (Mazelis, 1999)

- Arrest rates of trauma-exposed youth are up to eight times higher than community samples of same-age peers. (Saigh et al, 1999; Saltzman et al, 2001)

- Abused children are more likely to be in special education classes, have below-grade-level achievement test scores, exhibit poor work habits, and fail a grade. (Shonk, et al. 2001)

SIGNS OF TRAUMA

A. The experience of violence and victimization, including sexual abuse, severe neglect, loss, domestic violence and/or the witnessing of violence, terrorism, or disasters (NASMHPD, 2006)

B. Trauma is a psychologically distressing event outside the range of usual human experience. (Perry, 2002)

C. Trauma is an unusually severe stressor or event that causes or is capable of causing death, injury, or threat to physical integrity of self or others. (Baggerly, 2008)

D. Trauma is accompanied by intense feelings of horror, terror, or helplessness. (Baggerly, 2008)

E. Seriously threatens the health or survival of the individual

F. Renders the individual powerless in the face of overwhelming fear or arousal

G. Overwhelms the individual's coping capacity

H. Violates the basic assumptions about the safety of the environment and trusting others (Forrest-Perkins, 2011).

GLOSSARY OF TRAUMA-INFORMED TERMS

Burnout
Depletion of physical and intellectual energy

Compassion Fatigue
Emotional exhaustion that comes from "living" an individual's stresses, struggles, and fears day-in and day-out

Compassion Stress
Enduring negative psychological consequences of caregiver's exposure to the traumatic experiences of victims in their care (Schauben and Fraizer, 1995)

Counter-Transference
A condition where therapists and counselors, as a result of their therapy sessions, begin to transfer their own unconscious feelings to patients

Flashbacks
Trauma memories that have not been verbally integrated and come back in the form of sensory memories. They make it feel as if the traumas are occurring again in the here and now.

External Trauma
Experienced trauma such as war; being a crime victim; sudden natural death of a loved one; suicidal loss; loss of a loved one to homicide; sudden and unexpected loss of a job, housing, or relationship; living in extreme poverty; natural disasters, and accidents in vehicles, planes, trains, etc.

Historical Trauma
Cumulative emotional and psychological wounding resulting from trauma experienced by a social group. (e.g., slavery, Holocaust, etc.).

Interpersonal Trauma
Experienced trauma such as child abuse; sexual assault; historical trauma; domestic violence; loss due to homicide; torture and forcible confinement, and elder abuse

Sanctuary Trauma
The overt and covert traumatic events that occur in "trusted" institutions (e.g., medical, mental health and substance abuse facilities; correctional facilities; foster care; schools, and places of worship).

Therapeutic Relationship
An authentic, trusted relationship that is characterized by clear and concise boundaries fostered between trauma survivors and providers whereby respect, information, connection, and hope are paramount.

Transference
Generally refers to feelings and issues from the past that clients transfer or project onto the counselor/therapist/provider in their current relationship

Trauma Informed Care
An approach to engaging people with histories of trauma that recognizes the presence of trauma symptoms and acknowledges the role that trauma has played in peoples' lives. (NCTIC, 2013)

Trauma-Specific Services
A type of therapeutic intervention provided by a counselor with specialized knowledge and skills designed to treat trauma responses and adaptation and problematic substance use in an integrated manner. These services are significantly different from trauma-informed practices and methods. These services imply that an environment has been created in which trauma-informed practices are already implemented.

Trauma (Vicarious)
This is having empathy and engaging with trauma survivors and feeling responsible for them. It is important to be mindful of your internal responses to others' trauma.

Triggers
Flashbacks and trauma memories have not been verbally integrated and come back in the form of sensory memories making it feel as if the trauma were occurring again in the here and now. Triggers are identifiable situations or events that can create emotional upheaval.

Trauma Triggers
These flashbacks are most-often triggered by non-verbal memory, to wit:

- Sight
- Sounds
- Smells
- Bodily sensations
- Emotional reactions
- Motor memories

Simple Trauma

- Seeing, feeling, hearing, or smelling something that reminds us of past trauma
- Activating the alarm system
- Responding as if there is current danger.
- "Thinking brain" automatically shuts off in the face of triggers
- Past and present danger become confused

Complex Trauma

- More reminders of past danger
- Brain is more sensitive to danger
- Interactions with others often serve as triggers

Common Triggers

- Reminders of past events
- Lack of power/control
- Separation or loss
- Transitions and routine/schedule disruption
- Feelings of vulnerability and rejection
- Feeling threatened or attacked
- Sensory overload

RESOURCES AND REFERENCES

PUBLICATIONS

Bloom, S.L. (2005). Creating Sanctuary for Kids: Helping Children to Heal From Violence. Therapeutic Communities, 26(1), 54-60.

Cook, A., Blaustein, M., Spinazzola, J., & van der Kolk, B. (eds.) (2003). Complex Trauma in Children and adolescents. National Child Traumatic Stress Network. http://www.NCTSNet.org

Elliott, D.E., et al. (2005). Trauma-informed or Trauma-denied: Principles and Implementation of Trauma-informed Services for Women. Journal of Community Psychology. Vol. 33, No. 4.

Fallot, R. D. and Harris, M. (2001). A Trauma-Informed Approach to Screening and Assessment, Chapter 2 in New Directions for Mental Health Services, no. 89.

Fallot, R. D. and Harris, M. (2005). Integrated Trauma Services Teams for Women with Alcohol and Other Drug Problems and Co-occurring Mental Disorders. Alcoholism Treatment Quarterly. Vol. 22, 3-4.

Fallot, R. & Harris, M. (2009). Creating Cultures of Trauma-Informed Care: A self-assessment and planning protocol. Washington, DC: Community Connections.

Felitti, V.J., Anda., R.F., Nordenberg, D., Williamson, D.F., Spitz, A.M., Edwards, V., et. Al. (1998). Relationship of childhood abuse and household dysfunction to many of the leading causes of death in adults: The adverse childhood experiences (ACS) study. American Journal of Preventive Medicine, 14, 245-258.

Harris, M. & Fallot, R. (2001). Using Trauma Theory to Design Service Systems. San Francisco, CA: Jossey Bass.

Havig, K. (2008). The health care experience of adult survivor of sexual abuse: A system review of evidence on sensitive practice. Trauma, Violence, and Abuse, 9, 19-33.

Herman, J. (1992). Trauma and Recovery. New York, NY: Harper Collins.

Pearlman, L. A. and Saakvitne, K. W. (1995). Trauma and the Therapist: Countertransference and Vicarious Traumatization in Psychotherapy with Incest Survivors. New York: W. W. Norton & Company.

Perry, Bruce D., & Pollard, R. (1998). Homeostasis, stress, trauma, and adaption: A Neurodevelopmental View of Childhood Trauma. Child & Adolescent Psychiatric Clinics of North America, 7, 33-51.

Perry, Bruce. The Boy Who Was Raised as a Dog, p. 231-232. 30

Rich, J., et al. (2009). Healing the Hurt: Trauma-Informed Approaches to the Health of Boys and Young Men of Color. Philadelphia, PA: Drexell University School of Public Health; Drexel University College of Medicine; The California Endowment.

Seigel, D.J. (1999). The Developing Mind: Toward a Neurobiological of Interpersonal Experience. New York, NY: Guilford Press.

Prescott, L., et al. (2008). A Long Journey Home: A guide for generating trauma-informed services for mothers and children experiencing homelessness. Rockville, MD: Center for Mental Health Services, Substance Abuse and Mental Health Services Administration; Daniels Fund; National Child Traumatic Stress Network; W.K. Kellogg Foundation.

Prescott L, Soares P, Konnath K, Bassuk E. (2007). A long journey home: a guide for creating trauma-informed services for homeless mothers and children. Rockville, MD: Center for Mental Health Services, Substance Abuse and Mental Health Services Administration http://www.familyhomelessness.org/media/89.pdf

INTERNET RESOURCES

Adverse Child Experiences Study
www.acestudy.org

The Institute for Attachment and Child Development
www.instituteforattachment.org.

National Child Traumatic Stress Network
www.nctsn.org/

Trauma Center
www.traumacenter.org

Child Trauma Academy
www.childtraumaacademy.com/

National Child Traumatic Stress Network
www.nctsnet.org

National Center for PTSD
www.ncptsd.va.gov

National Clearinghouse for Child Abuse and Neglect (NCCAN)
www.nccanch.acf.hhs.gov

Prevent Child Abuse, America
www.preventchildabuse.org/index.shtml

Clinic Community Health Centre: Trauma-informed Toolkit
www.trauma-informed.ca

ABOUT THE AUTHOR
TONIER CAIN

Tonier Cain works tirelessly to raise the awareness about trauma informed care around the world. She has trained providers in all 50 states. Tonier is an advocate and educator, speaking all overthe world on trauma, addiction, incarceration, homelessness, substance abuse and mental health. Her work has been used as a model in other countries for the establishment of their trauma informed care protocols.

Tonier was the former team leader for the *National Center for Trauma Informed Care,* with the *National Association of State Mental Health* Program Director. Currently she works to create international leaders in the field of Trauma Informed Care. She hosts an annual national conference to update and enlighten providers on current best practices. Tonier's methods have proven to be effective, resulting in numerous awards for her work. She has been honored by two governors, a mayor and a state attorney with proclamations naming days after her, because of her help to transform their city and state.

Tonier is the C.E.O. and Founder of *Tonier Cain International,* Founder and President of *Neen Cares, Inc.* A 501 C 3, Founder and Co-C.E.O. of *M.E.T.-R Integrated Health Global,* as well as the Founder and C.E.O. of *Purposeful Entertainment,* a production company.

She is an award winning Film Producer that is the Creator and Producer of the upcoming TV show *Restoration,* Executive Producer of the film *Walking Thru Bullets,* subject and Co-Producer of the award-winning film *Healing Neen,* along being featured in the documentary *Behind Closed Doors: Trauma Survivors in the Psychiatrist Syst*em, and advising on the film *Like Any Other Kid.*

Tonier is an author and serves as a *Citygate Network* Board Member. Her commitment to advocating for those who are often forgotten hasn't gone without recognition. She has been featured in many articles including December's 2014 *Ebony Magazine* and appeared on over 17 talks shows. Tonier Cain uses her life experiences to make a difference for trauma survivors.

HOPE

For booking information, email
hello@toniercain.com

www.toniercain.com

Follow us on social media,
@toniercain

Made in United States
Troutdale, OR
04/17/2024

19255710R00076